BIBLE STORIES

for

SMALL GROUPS

Michael L. Leno

BIBLE STORIES

for

SMALL GROUPS

Michael L. Leno

Pacific Press Publishing Association
Boise, Idaho
Oshawa, Ontario, Canada

Edited by B. Russell Holt
Designed by Dennis Ferree
Cover by Dennis Ferree
Typeset in 10/12 Times Roman

Library of Congress Cataloging-in-Publication Data
Leno, Michael L., 1954-
   Bible stories for small groups: exploring biblical relationships / Michael L. Leno.
         p.   cm.
   Includes bibliographical references
   ISBN 0-8163-1028-9
   1. Bible—Study—Textbooks. I. Title
BS605.2.L465   1991
220'.076—dc20   91-12715
                                                          CIP

91 92 93 94 95 • 5 4 3 2 1

Table of Contents

Introduction

The stories in the Bible aren't ''kid's stuff''! Of course, kids need to learn Bible stories, but the real, contemporary dilemmas that adults face day to day are what the Bible is all about. Who else but grown-ups can appreciate David's situation when caught between spouse, in-laws, country, and religion? Who else can really understand the way Jesus handled the Pharisees when they asked Him to pass judgment on a woman caught sleeping around?

You may be startled to discover facts and ideas in the Bible stories that were never explained when you were a kid. For instance, what was Saul *really* doing in the cave when David cut a piece out of his robe? (He wasn't taking a nap!) And why were Job's friends dead wrong when they were just trying to defend God's honor?

Whether you've heard these stories a thousand times or whether this is your first time, you'll find them to be some of the most awesome, spine-tingling, funny, tear-jerking, romantic, and all-around wonderful stories ever told. More important, in this series of studies you will discover God in a way you may not have imagined possible. As you talk and listen with your study group, you'll also discover that God is still working today. Who says kids get to have all the interesting stuff?

What happens in a small group?

If you have never joined a weekly small group, you are in for a surprise. Such groups do more than just discuss points of view. A small group does three things:

1. It forms a bond, a true fellowship, among the group members.

With time, your group will become a Christian support group. In order for this to happen, group members must commit themselves to meeting every week.

2. It provides a *relational* Bible study. This is not the type of study in which one person does all the teaching. Neither is it the type in which everyone participates by giving his or her opinion on a certain topic. Relational Bible study focuses on feelings as well as knowledge. Rather than trying to convince the group of a particular viewpoint, your leader will encourage group members to affirm each other and to express how the scripture passages apply to their own lives.

3. It reaches out to new members. When you discover a good thing, it's natural to share it. Many groups go even further and plan special projects that share the gospel in a tangible way.

Even though you can use these studies on an individual basis, studying with a group of four to twelve people can give you the most benefit. There's always a period of adjustment at first, particularly if several group members have not experienced this type of study. Learning to trust each other and the God of Scripture is what study and fellowship groups are all about.

You are about to begin an adventure!

Leading a Small Group

Getting started—don't make it complicated!

Leading a small group presents the same dilemma as does getting a job—you need experience in order to do the job, but you need to do the job in order to get experience! Education, training, apprenticeship, etc., can solve the problem partially, but these can never substitute for experience. So don't make it complicated—dive right in! The best possible way to get started in small group study is simply to join a group. If there is no group available to you, get a small group of friends together and start one.

With this book as a guide, you can start a group whether or not you have training or experience. Nevertheless, as a leader, you will want some training in addition to your small-group experience. Training will not only acquaint you with the experiences and methods of other small groups but will prepare you for many of the potential pitfalls common to the life cycle of small groups. Many churches have small-group training available. (The Oregon Conference of Seventh-day Adventists has published some very good material on small groups.) The Serendipity workshops by Lyman Coleman are some of the best, and probably the most available, training you will find. Ask the Christian bookstore in your area for a schedule or write to the address given at the end of this chapter. Take your entire group to a training session!

Breaking the ice

Your group's first meeting is extremely important. Therefore, you must understand your role as leader. In the early sessions you will probably have to do more talking than the other individuals in the group. As time goes on, however, you should become less prominent and act as a facilitator.

From the beginning, you must establish a relational study style. You may need some "icebreakers" to get the group to start sharing *themselves,* not just exchanging ideas and opinions. Below are some ideas to get you started. They are not necessarily deep questions, so don't spend too much time on them—ten to fifteen minutes is usually enough. As time goes on, the group members will learn to feel comfortable sharing what is really happening to them spiritually. The masks will come off, and your group will become a valuable source of Christian support.

Your immediate goal is to create a group environment in which people are secure with each other. As your group matures, the icebreakers become less important, although your group may still enjoy them.

Icebreakers for small groups

1. Four Quaker Questions:

● Where were you living between the ages of seven and twelve . . . and what were the winters like?

● How did you heat your house during this time?

● What was the center of warmth in your life during this time? (This can be a place in the house, a time of year, or a person.)

● When did God become a "warm" person to you, and how did it happen?[1]

2. If you received one million dollars cash, tax free, what would you do with it? How would it change you?

3. Describe what your house will be like in the new earth. Who do you want to visit you (family, friends, historical or biblical characters)?

4. Choose *one* of the two songs that would best describe how you are feeling right now about that area for your life:

● In my personal life, I'm feeling:

"Blues in the Night"   "Feelin' Groovy"

● In my family life, I'm feeling:

"Stormy Weather"   "The Sound of Music"

● In my work or career, I'm feeling:
"Take This Job and Shove It"   "Everything's Coming Up Roses"

● In my spiritual life, I'm feeling:
"Mickey Mouse Disco"   "Hallelujah Chorus"

● In my relationships, I'm feeling:
"Nowhere Man"   "You Light Up My Life"

● As I look at the future, I'm feeling:
"Yesterday"   "To Dream the Impossible Dream"[2]

5. If you could create the ideal place to live, what ingredients would you need—people, climate, location, etc.? For instance, you might need the beaches of Hawaii, the friends you had in high school, the ski slopes of Austria, and live in a houseboat on the river. (It doesn't have to be logical!)

6. What item in your billfold or purse is the most valuable to you? Why?

7. If your house caught fire and you could rescue just two things (besides your family members), what would they be?

8. What famous person, living or dead, would you like to visit with? What would you ask him or her?

9. Describe an embarrassing situation in your life.

10. What was the most unusual thing your mother (or grandmother, aunt, etc.) carried in her purse?

Group commitment

A successful group must have a six- to eight-week commitment from each of its members. You may ask the members of your group to commit themselves before coming. Or you may have one or two introductory sessions and then make the commitment together. In any case, except for the unavoidable and unforeseen, each member must feel responsible to attend the group each week for the specified number of sessions.

Relate, Don't Debate

Typical group discussions often end up in debate—one side versus the other. Even when no sides emerge, groups that discuss only ideas have little to do except agree or disagree. In the right environment, a good intellectual discussion can be enjoyable and healthy. But when discussion turns to debating, it prevents secure, relational group interaction. A good rule of thumb is: *Do not allow the group to focus on either doctrine or politics!* Both are important, but your small group is not the place to settle these kinds of issues.

What do you do with a theological logjam? Suppose someone in your group suddenly takes the floor and proclaims that speaking in tongues is the only way to be part of the New Testament church? And suppose that in response, the members of your group start arguing with him?

Here's another rule of thumb: Talk about your own feelings, not about what someone else should or shouldn't feel. Encourage each of your group members to share how the scripture passage relates to him or her. Encourage honest, nonjudgmental-feeling statements. An example in this case might be: "I feel elated when I hear the story of the day of Pentecost." Or, "The way God worked through Peter so powerfully makes me feel hopeful that it could happen again." The group can then affirm these statements without having to agree or disagree with anyone. This kind of study not only builds relationships but allows the Bible to speak directly to people. Group members learn what the Bible teaches, not what the group leader teaches.

Why are feeling statements important? Shouldn't we steer clear of feelings and get down to clear-headed thinking unclouded by emotions? We should always be as clear-headed as possible, but we also have to recognize that feelings are always present, whether or not we acknowledge them. In fact, trying not to acknowledge them may allow them to dominate us. We should also realize that while logic may drive discussions, feelings drive relationships. It won't matter how correct you are; if someone has a bad feeling about you, the relationship will suffer.

If all else fails, simply return the attention of the group to the questions in the lesson. Most of them are designed to help your group relate, not debate.

Celebrations

Celebrations help your group become even more caring and supportive. Use special times such as birthdays and anniversaries to affirm each other. Make a six- or eight-week commitment to each other, and have a celebration at the end.

Celebrate communion in your group. Your pastor may even want to encourage all the small groups in your congregation to do this on a regular basis.

The possibilities are endless. The most available, and perhaps the most important, is the weekly Sabbath celebration. Make the church service a special event for your group. If some in your group do not attend church, a nonthreatening invitation can be one more way to strengthen your relationship with them. Find a special job or ministry on Sabbath morning that your group can do together!

Information about Serendipity
Serendipity House
Box 1012
Littleton, CO 80160
1-800-525-9563

---

1. *Small Group Bible Studies, Basics* (Littleton, Colo.: Serendipity House, 1983).
2. Ibid.

BIBLE
STORIES
for
SMALL
GROUPS

Story #1—Abraham and Isaac
Faith Beyond the Limit

Why join a group?

Good question! After all, most of us are capable of studying on our own. This group will mean more to all of us than study, however. There are two things (at least) that one cannot do alone: get married and be a Christian! So first of all, realize that people need you. Even if you sit like a bump on a log, you are there, and that's more important than you realize! Second, realize that you need a group of supportive people who will commit themselves to each other. Sure, it may be a little awkward at times, and it will definitely take a lot of commitment for everyone to meet once a week, but the results will be well worth the effort.

Since this is a group study, you will gain the most from this experience if you follow several guidelines:

    a. Study the story lesson before your group study.
    b. Be faithful in attending your group.
    c. Spend time at each group study to simply get acquainted.
    d. Pray for your group members.
    e. Celebrate with everyone each Sabbath.

Background

Read Genesis 15:1-6; 16:1-15; 17:1-22; and 21:1-13. Now focus on the story in chapter 22. You may wish to read the entire life story of Abraham. It begins in chapter 12 and ends in chapter 25.

Chapter 16

1. What do you think of the surrogate relationship of Hagar and Sarah? Was this the "easy way out"? What pressures was Abraham facing? What were Sarah's motives?

2. What might change your opinion of Abraham and Sarah—
   a. knowing it was a common cultural practice in their day for childless couples to include as their own any children the man had by his servants?
   b. knowing their attitude and motives were right toward God?
   c. knowing Sarah was now seventy-seven and had always been barren?
   d. knowing it had been ten years since God promised them a son?

3. What are some modern motives for sexual intimacy outside marriage?

Chapter 22

4. What made this test more significant than any other test Abraham may have had?

5. Have circumstances ever forced you to choose between your family and your convictions?

6. Which of the following would be hardest for you to give up for God?

Children	Parents
TV	Health
Friends	Religious beliefs
Reputation	Independence
Career	Sex appeal
Church membership	Spouse

7. Why do you think Abraham passed the test?
   a. He took a blind leap of faith.
   b. He was afraid of not obeying God.
   c. He knew God well enough to trust Him.
   d. He didn't love his family very much.
   e. He didn't consult his family.

> "The sacrifice of human beings, particularly of infants, was common in ancient times. Both the Bible and archaeology affirm that the Canaanites practiced such rites. The idea of sacrificing one's firstborn to the deity was therefore nothing strange to Abraham. While God explicitly prohibited such sacrifices (Lev. 18:21), it is not certain that Abraham was clear as to this. Indeed, only on the assumption that he did not understand this divine ban can we explain his failure to protest God's command to offer up his son."[2]

8. After it was all over, how do you think Isaac felt about his dad? Do you think Isaac had a "martyr complex"?

9. Have you ever felt "laid on the altar" for someone else's cause? How did you deal with it?

10. What do you look for most in your study group?
   a. Intellectual challenge.
   b. Emotional support.
   c. Friends.
   d. Bible knowledge.
   e. Get away from the rat race and relax.
   f. Encouragement to study for myself.
   g. ________________________________.

The next in this series of Bible stories is found in the book of Job.

1. *The NIV Serendipity Bible* (Grand Rapids, Mich.: Zondervan, 1988), p. 56.
2. *SDA Bible Commentary* (Washington, D.C.: Review and Herald, 1976, 1977), vol. 1, p. 350.

Story #2—Job

Does God Put Us Through Hell?

Background

Read the book of Job, preferably using a modern version such as the New International Version, Today's English Version, or the Revised Standard Version.

Job's story

1. The story of Job takes place on two levels. Only at the end of the story do these two levels come together. Does this relate to your life in any way?

Heavenly level—God talks to Satan

God talks to Job and friends

Earthly level—Job suffers, talks to friends

2. Is Job aware of what is happening in heaven? Does he seem aware of Satan's existence or activities on earth?

The following is a condensation of the conversations in the book of Job.

Job's arguments

Why did I have to live?
I'm innocent, so why does God treat me this way?
God is the only one I can trust—even if it costs me my life!

20

My friends give me miserable comfort and long-winded sermons! If
   they are right, God has wronged me!
I know that my redeemer/defender lives and will set things right.
Why do the wicked live on?

Job's friends' arguments

Don't despise God's discipline.
Your children got their just reward.
God is giving you less punishment than you deserve!
You are sinful; that's why you suffer.
God considers you but a worm or a maggot.
God can't reward you unless you repent.

God answers Job

Job, remember you don't know everything.
There are many things beyond your control—stars, wild beasts, etc.

Job answers God

I spoke of things I did not understand.
My ears had heard of You, but now my eyes have seen You.
I repent.

God answers Job's friends

You have not told the truth about Me as Job has!
Job will pray for you, and I will accept his prayer.

Reflect

3. Describe a situation in which someone tried to comfort or help
you but only made you feel worse. Have you ever made a situation
worse by giving advice? How do you react to advice when you are
hurting?

4. What would you want your friends to say to you if you were
hurting or grieving? What's the worst thing they could say?
   a. It was God's will.
   b. God doesn't give us more than we can bear.
   c. God lets things happen to make us stronger.
   d. Bad things happen to people who don't trust God.
   e. Everything happens for a reason.

    f. There is no reason for what happened.
    g. God is grieving too.
    h. God is just as outraged as you are.

5. In what way is God on trial in the story of Job?

6. What is the worst thing that has ever happened to you? Did you ever feel as Job did in chapter 3? How did the experience change you?

7. In what kind of God did Job's friends believe? In what way did Job say what was right about God (see Job 42:7)?

8. Does God cause the bad things that happen to us? What does Job's "happy ending" represent in your life?

9. What kind of friends do you need most right now?
    a. Smart—they can give you the answers you need.
    b. Feeling—they care about your feelings.
    c. Honest—even if it hurts.
    d. Close to God—they know what kind of person God is.
    e. ____.

How seriously would we take a person who said, "I have faith in Adolf Hitler or in John Dillinger? I can't explain why they did the things they did, but I can't believe they would have done them without a good reason"? Yet people try to justify the deaths and tragedies God inflicts on innocent victims with almost these same words.[1]

There may be another approach. Maybe God does not cause our suffering. Maybe it happens for some reason other than the will of God.[2]

The next in this series of Bible stories is found in 1 Samuel 24-26.

---

1. Harold S. Kushner, *When Bad Things Happen to Good People* (New York: Avon Books, 1981), p. 19.
2. Ibid., p. 29.

Loving the Enemy—and Winning!

The story of Saul begins in 1 Samuel 8, when Israel asks to have a king for the first time in its history. Saul becomes the first king and is very successful until chapter 15, when he goes against God's instructions. David enters the story in chapter 16, when he is anointed to be the next king. He kills Goliath in chapter 17 and thus sets the stage for several confrontations with jealous King Saul, whose power is declining. Saul dies in battle in chapter 31.

Read as much of the story of David and Saul as you have time for. Focus on 1 Samuel chapters 24 to 26.

Chapter 24

1. Have any authority figures (parents, teachers, bosses, etc.) in your past betrayed or disappointed you? How did you handle it? Would you do the same today?

2. With whom do you identify in this story?
   a. Saul—frustrated because he can't keep up with all his problems and scared to face himself.
   b. David—unjustly harassed, caught between what works and what is "right."
   c. David's men—living on the edge, seeing a God-sent opportunity slipping through their fingers.

3. What are the implications of verse 22 for loving your enemies?

Chapter 25

4. If you are married, describe how you met your spouse.

5. What does your spouse (or best friend) do that is most helpful when you are angry?

6. Do you think Abigail was:
   a. Acting the part of a peacemaker?
   b. Just saving her property and possibly her life?
   c. Trying to save her husband's life?
   d. Flirting with David?
   e. Manipulative?
   f. God's way of teaching David something?
   g. _______________________________

> **"Abishai.** The grandson of Jesse. Abishai was the son of David's sister, Zeruiah, and therefore David's nephew. Abishai's brother, Joab (1 Chron. 2:16), was the leader of David's forces."[1]

Chapter 26

7. Why did David say what he did in verse 10?
   a. He really wanted to kill Saul, but he was afraid of what God would do if he did.
   b. It was the only way to convince Abishai to do what was right.
   c. It was David's way of saying that those who live by the sword die by the sword (see Matthew 26:54). (There are natural, inevitable results of sin.)

8. How is David different in this chapter, compared to the cave experience in chapter 24?

9. How does David love Saul, even though he can't trust him?

10. Have you ever been "burned" a second time by someone? How did you react?

11. How would you describe David's philosophy?
   a. Forgive twice; three strikes, and they're out!

b. Keep loving even if you get burned.
c. Forgive, but don't enable.
d. Hang in there; it has to get better!
e. What goes around, comes around.
f. Nice guys finish best!

12. Tell the members of your group why you think they are winners. The members of the group should take turns being silent while the rest of the group talks about them in this affirming way. Share how you feel when you finish this exercise.

"David could not be present at the burial of Samuel, but he mourned for him as deeply and tenderly as a faithful son could mourn for a devoted father. . . . While the attention of Saul was engaged in mourning for the death of Samuel, David took the opportunity to seek a place of greater security; so he fled to the wilderness of Paran. It was here that he composed the one-hundred-twentieth and twenty-first psalms. In these desolate wilds, realizing that the prophet was dead, and the king was his enemy, he sang:"[2]

> My help comes from the Lord,
>   the Maker of heaven and earth.
> he will not let your foot slip—
>   he who watches over you will not slumber;
> indeed, he who watches over Israel
>   will neither slumber nor sleep. . . .
> The Lord will keep you from all harm—
>   he will watch over your life;
> the Lord will watch over your coming and going
>   both now and forevermore.
>
> Psalm 121:2-8 (NIV).

The next in this series of Bible stories is found in 2 Samuel, chapters 11 and 12.

---

1. *SDA Bible Commentary* (Washington, D.C.: Review and Herald, 1976, 1978), vol. 2, p. 577.
2. Ellen G. White, *Patriarchs and Prophets* (Boise, Idaho: Pacific Press), p. 664.

Story #4—David and Bathsheba

Love, Indifference, and Grace

The story of David and Bathsheba is found in 2 Samuel, chapters 11 and 12. If possible, read some of the chapters leading up to this story to get a flavor of what has happened in David's life. As you will see, David was at the height of his power. Never before or since has the nation of Israel been in such complete control of that part of the world.

The Bible does not blush at telling the truth about its heroes. They are presented as the fallible human beings they were. While it might be easier for us not to talk about such subjects as sexual sin and murder, the Bible's record of real life shows a God who is capable of dealing with any problem and healing any wound.

Chapter 11

1. Was David ''ripe'' for such a temptation? What evidence do you see of a possible ''midlife crisis''?

2. How would this be a tempting situation for Bathsheba?

3. What does this chapter imply about the place of women at this time? What about the ''rights'' of kings?

4. What was the worst thing David did?
    a. Go AWOL.
    b. Lust after a foreign woman?
    c. Commit adultery (seventh commandment).

    d. Involve Joab in his plot.
    e. Deceive Uriah (ninth commandment).
    f. Plot to kill Uriah (sixth commandment).
    g. Covet his neighbor's wife (tenth commandment).[1]

5. How does this story end?
    a. "Happily ever after."
    b. The beginning of the end.
    c. Appearances are deceiving.
    d. God has the final word.[2]

6. Faced with similar circumstances, what makes you feel vulnerable to temptation?
    a. The grass is always greener.
    b. I like a challenge.
    c. Sometimes I do really stupid things.
    d. I always want more.
    e. If God ever left me, I'd be helpless.[3]

7. I could be more faithful to my spouse and family by:
    a. Being more of a spiritual leader.
    b. Realizing that the grass is *not* greener elsewhere.
    c. Being a better listener.
    d. Rearranging my schedule.
    e. Keeping my promises.
    f. Letting them know I love them by _____________________.

"When kings go forth. The rulers of Western Asia generally started out on their military campaigns in the spring of the year. The winter was unsuited for fighting because of the cold and the rain. Also the roads at that time were well-nigh impassable and supplies of food were not readily available. The Assyrian annals show that almost invariably the spring of the year was chosen for the armies to conduct their campaigns. With the Assyrians, these were annual expeditions."[4]

Chapter 12

8. How was Nathan tactful but direct?

9. How do you regard the Nathans in your life?
    a. I'm glad when they're tactful.
    b. I have a hard time recognizing them.
    c. They make me angry.
    d. I'm glad I don't have their job!
    e. I wish they'd leave me alone.
    f. I'm glad when someone cares enough to confront me.

10. This story is good news for me because:
    a. Now I know that there's hope for anyone.
    b. I see how God corrects in love.
    c. I see that even the greatest Bible heroes had faults.
    d. I know that just because I blow it, it doesn't have to be the end.
    e. ____.

"Many have murmured at what they called God's injustice in sparing David, whose guilt was so great, after having rejected Saul for what appeared to them to be far less flagrant sins. But David humbled himself and confessed his sin, while Saul despised reproof and hardened his heart in impenitence."[5]

The next in this series of Bible stories is found in the book of Jonah.

---

1. *The NIV Serendipity Bible*, p. 413.
2. Ibid.
3. Ibid.
4. *SDA Bible Commentary* (Washington, D.C.: Review and Herald, 1976), vol. 2, p. 646.
5. Ellen G. White, *Patriarchs and Prophets* (Boise, Idaho: Pacific Press), p. 726.

Story #5—Jonah

Remade in the Shade!

The story of Jonah is famous as a big fish story. There's a lot more to the story, however, than just an aquatic nightmare! Read the book of Jonah in as many different translations as you can and try to empathize with Jonah. As you share with your study and fellowship group, try to bring the experience of Jonah into our time.

Chapter 1

1. I feel most like running away when:
    a. The sewer backs up.
    b. I feel exploited.
    c. I feel underpaid and overworked.
    d. I can't seem to get ahead.
    e. My sense of purpose is gone.
    f. I face drastic changes.
    g. My self-worth is in the pits.

2. Why do you think Jonah could sleep through the storm?
    a. God put him in a deep sleep.
    b. He could escape from himself as well as God.
    c. He was tired.
    d. It was easier than facing reality.
    e. ____ .

3. In what way were the sailors in a double bind? What kind of

god(s) did they believe in?

Chapter 2

4. Describe a time when you wanted God to get you out of a jam. Did you promise God anything? How does God regard "foxhole" conversions?

5. Why does Jonah sound so thankful in this chapter?

Chapter 3

6. How do you feel about Jonah's "gospel" preaching? How do you think Jonah felt about it?

7. Knowing that Nineveh would later return to its wicked ways, how do you feel about its conversion in this chapter? How does God feel about it?

Chapter 4

8. When I'm angry at God:
    a. I never admit it.
    b. God uses it to help me grow.
    c. I'm afraid God is angry at me.
    d. It's because I let God down.
    e. It's because God let me down.
    f. People usually condemn me.

> **You have been concerned (verse 10).** "Jonah, the angry and unsympathetic prophet, was willing to show pity and spare an inconsequential gourd of little value, and upon which he had expended no labor or toil, but was unwilling to show the same consideration to the people of the great city of Nineveh. The LXX renders the first part of the verse, 'And the Lord said, Thou hadst pity on the gourd, for which thou hast not suffered, neither didst thou rear it.' . . . Jonah cared more for the gourd than for the people of Nineveh."[1]

9. What was God's real intention when He sent Jonah with a forty-

day "eviction notice" to Nineveh? Have you ever felt like a "false prophet"?

    10. I find it hard to love and accept people when:
        a. They've already had a second chance.
        b. They belong to a group I distrust. (Communists, Catholics, Adventists, Arabs, Japanese, Jews, Liberals, Conservatives, _________?)
        c. They disagree with me.
        d. They don't love and accept me.
        e. They don't practice what they preach.

    11. How has God given you a second (or third, fourth, fifth . . .) chance?

"Among the cities of the ancient world in the days of divided Israel one of the greatest was Nineveh, the capital of the Assyrian realm. Founded on the fertile bank of the Tigris, soon after the dispersion from the tower of Babel, it had flourished through the centuries until it had become 'an exceeding great city of three day's journey.' Jonah 3:3.

"In the time of its temporal prosperity Nineveh was a center of crime and wickedness. Inspiration has characterized it as 'the bloody city, . . . full of lies and robbery.' In figurative language the prophet Nahum compared the Ninevites to a cruel, ravenous lion. 'Upon whom,' he inquired, 'hath not thy wickedness passed continually?' Nahum 3:1, 19."[2]

The next in this series of Bible stories is found in the book of Nehemiah, particularly chapters 1-6, 8, 9, and 12.

---

1. *SDA Bible Commentary*, vol. 4, p. 1007.
2. Ellen G. White, *Prophets and Kings* (Boise, Idaho: Pacific Press, p. 265.

Story #6—Nehemiah

You Can Do the Impossible!

Background: Read the entire book of Nehemiah. Focus on chapters 1-6, 8, and 9.

The books of Ezra and Nehemiah cover the return of Israel after the seventy years of Babylonian captivity.

"This is accomplished through the help of three Persian kings (Cyrus, Darius, and Artaxerxes I). Cyrus was an enlightened king who reversed the oppressive policies of his Assyrian and Babylonian predecessors and encouraged the return of the exiles and the rebirth of their religion. There is some question as to when Ezra and Nehemiah reached Jerusalem. However, the traditional view is that Ezra arrived in Jerusalem in the seventh year of the reign of Artaxerxes I (458 B.C.) and Nehemiah in the twentieth year of that reign (445 B.C.)."[1]

Ezra's leadership sparked a revival among the returned captives, and they started rebuilding the walls around Jerusalem. When hardship and opposition halted the restoration, Nehemiah, as an official governor appointed by Artaxerxes I, organized and motivated God's people to finish the task.

Chapters 1-3

1. Have you ever "come home" after being away a long time? How had things changed? How were things the same?

2. Where are you in your spiritual history: in captivity? returning? rebuilding? discouraged? in dedication and celebration?

3. Compare Ezra 8:22, 23 with Nehemiah 2:7-9. Do you think the fact that Ezra was a religious leader and Nehemiah a political leader explains their different attitudes toward government aid? Do you think one was right and the other wrong? Did one have more faith than the other?

4. What are some "walls" in your life that could be built with a little cooperation?

5. Why is each person in your group an important part of the "wall-building team"? (Go around the circle in your group as the rest of the group affirms the value of each person in turn.)

Chapters 4-6
6. Which kind of opposition is hardest for you to deal with? Why?
   a. Competitors who want you to fail.
   b. Disapproving friends or neighbors.
   c. Well-meaning but negative church members.
   d. Jealous or discouraged family members.

7. What do you learn from Nehemiah about dealing with opposition?

Chapters 8, 9
8. What do you do when you realize how imperfect you are?
   a. Try harder.
   b. Give up.
   c. Wish God would tell me it's all right.
   d. Wish I had something to celebrate.
   e. Confess and ask forgiveness.

9. What does Nehemiah 8:9-12 tell you about the kind of person God is?

10. Why is it important to mix praise and confession as in chapter 9?

11. Sum up the elements of Nehemiah's strategy that enabled him to do the "impossible."

12. Why are church services a celebration for you? In what ways might they need changing in order to help you celebrate, deal with guilt, learn what God is like, feel close to fellow believers, etc.?

"It is the first and highest duty of every rational being to learn from the Scriptures what is truth, and then to walk in the light. . . . With divine help we are to form our opinions for ourselves as we are to answer for ourselves before God."[2]

The next in this series of Bible stories is found in John 8:1-11.

---

1. *The NIV Serendipity Bible*, p. 598.
2. Ellen G. White, *The Great Controversy*, p. 598.

Story #7—The Woman Caught in Adultery
Love on the Rocks

The story

"The woman caught in adultery" is really the story of an attempt to trap Jesus. Jesus, of course, not only cleverly avoids the trap, but shows His compassion and forgiveness for the woman who was also entrapped. While we do not know the name of the woman involved, some have suspected that Mary Magdalene, Mary the sister of Lazarus and Martha, and this woman could in fact be the same person. Whether this is actually true is irrelevant. The point is, it is helpful to study these other cases to get a fuller picture of Jesus' attitudes and methods.

Read this story in John 8:1-11 and also the passages in Matthew 26:6-13; Mark 14:3-11; Luke 7:36-50; John 11:55-57; 12:1-11; and Luke 8:2.

1. Have you ever been caught without an excuse?

2. Have you ever received forgiveness when you knew you deserved none? How did you feel?

3. What might have happened if:
    a. Jesus had told the Pharisees to forgive her?
    b. Jesus had told the Pharisees to stone her?
    c. Jesus had told the Pharisees to leave her alone?

4. What similarities do you see between the Old Testament prophet, Jonah, and the Pharisees in Jesus' day?

5. I think the Pharisees were motivated by:
   a. Concern for their own popularity.
   b. A desire to "clean up the church."
   c. A misunderstanding of God's law.
   d. A desire to destroy Jesus' credibility.

6. Why do you think Jesus responded by writing on the ground?
   a. To avoid a shouting match.
   b. To avoid playing into the authority of the woman's accusers.
   c. To buy some time.
   d. To make the accusers think about their own lives.
   e. To make the crowd think instead of just reacting.
   f. To take control of the situation.

7. Why do you suspect the older accusers left first (verse 9)?
   a. The older ones knew of more sins in their own lives.
   b. The younger ones took longer to catch on.
   c. The more mature would be less judgmental.
   d. The younger ones were the most anxious to prove they could trap Jesus.
   e. ____

8. Who is the hardest for you to forgive?
   a. A child abuser.
   b. A war criminal.
   c. Someone who cheats on their spouse.
   d. A church leader who steals from the members.
   e. A drug pusher.

9. If you could hear Jesus say directly to you, "I don't condemn you; you are free to leave your life of sin," how would you feel?
   a. Guilty and ashamed.
   b. Relieved but anxious to please Him.
   c. More alive and free than ever before.
   d. Afraid to fail again.
   e. Like jumping for joy.
   f. ____.

10. What obstacles do you find within yourself when forgiving?

a. People don't apologize or seem very sorry.
b. I'm too angry to forgive.
c. I'm afraid I'll be taken advantage of.
d. I've never felt fully forgiven.
e. _______________________________________.

11. On a scale of one to ten, how good are you at forgiving yourself? Where would you like to be?

1   2   3   4   5   6   7   8   9   10

I never forgive myself   I always forgive myself

12. When you realize that God the Father is the same kind of person as Jesus the Son, how does this story help you relate to the Father? Is it hard for you to think of the Father in the same way as Jesus? Why?

"Jesus knows the circumstances of every soul. You may say, I am sinful, very sinful. You may be; but the worse you are, the more you need Jesus. He turns no weeping, contrite one away. He does not tell to any all that He might reveal, but He bids every trembling soul take courage. Freely will He pardon all who come to Him for forgiveness and restoration."[1]

The next in this series of Bible stories is found in Matthew 26:14-75; 27:1-10.

---

1. Ellen G. White, *The Desire of Ages* (Boise, Idaho: Pacific Press), p. 568.

Story #8—Peter and Judas
Jesus' Two Betrayers

The story

Read the following texts: Matthew 26:14-75; 27:1-10; Mark 14:27-72; Luke 22:1-62; John 13:18-38; 18:1-27; 21:1-19.

This study of Peter and Judas focuses on the contrasts and similarities between these two and their relationship to Jesus. You should read not only this story but the larger context as well, which includes the Last Supper; Jesus' trial, death, and resurrection; and His postresurrection appearances.

Comparison and contrast

1. Notice the discussion in Mark 10:35-45 and its parallel reference in Luke 22:24. How many disciples had selfish motives?

2. Compare Matthew 26:6-13 with John 12:1-8. How are the attitudes of Judas and the rest of the disciples apparently similar? How did Judas differ from the others?

3. What similarities and/or differences do you notice about Peter and Judas in the following texts? Matthew 16:21-23; Luke 22:1-6; John 13:37, 38; Luke 22:47, 48; Luke 22:61, 62; Matthew 27:1-5.

4. What do you think was:
   a. Judas's main strength?
   b. Judas's main weakness?
   c. Peter's main strength?

d. Peter's main weakness?

5. After denying or betraying Jesus, how were the confessions of Peter and Judas similar and/or different? Which one felt worse?

6. Why would the experience in John 21:1-19 help Peter deal with his guilt? How would it help him have a purpose in life and bring out his full potential in the future?

Application

7. My natural tendency is to be like:
   a. Peter: Promise God more than I can deliver and then ask for forgiveness.
   b. Judas: Know exactly what I can deliver and be hard on myself when I fail.

8. Describe a situation in which you were among people who verbally or nonverbally kept trying to compete with each other. How does this game of ''one-upmanship'' affect relationships? What do you think Jesus would say to the group you just described?

9. Judging from the way Jesus treated the disciples, especially Peter and Judas, how does God treat people with "known sin" in their lives?
   a. He keeps them on probation until they change.
   b. Only perfect people can be in His presence.
   c. He keeps giving them opportunities to grow.
   d. He never stops loving and forgiving and accepting.
   e. He doesn't help them if they haven't repented yet.
   f. God is not always as forgiving and patient as Jesus was with the disciples.
   g. The experience of the disciples is not applicable to us because we live so near the end of time.
   h. The life of Jesus is the clearest picture of the way God has always been and always will be.

10. When I try to make things right with God:
    a. I feel He expects just the right words and actions before He accepts me.
    b. I know He has accepted me already; it's just hard to feel it.
    c. I feel I have to punish myself and feel really bad before I can

feel better again.

    d. I project the attitudes of my earthly parents onto my heavenly Father.

    e. I'm able to accept forgiveness and acceptance without reservation and without feeling as if I have to earn it.

> "Had God the Father come to our world and dwelt among us, humbling Himself, veiling His glory, that humanity might look upon Him, the history that we have of the life of Christ would not have been changed. . . . In every act of Jesus, in every lesson of His instruction, we are to see and hear and recognize God. In sight, in hearing, in effect, it is the voice and movements of the Father."[1]

"The apostles differed widely in habits and disposition. There were the publican, Levi-Matthew, and the fiery zealot Simon, the uncompromising hater of the authority of Rome; the generous, impulsive Peter, and the mean-spirited Judas; Thomas, truehearted, yet timid and fearful; Philip, slow of heart, and inclined to doubt; and the ambitious, outspoken sons of Zebedee, with their brethren. These were brought together, with their different faults, all with inherited and cultivated tendencies to evil; but in and through Christ they were to dwell in the family of God, learning to become one in faith, in doctrine, in spirit. They would have their tests, their grievances, their differences of opinion; but while Christ was abiding in the heart, there could be no dissension. His love would lead to love for one another; the lessons of the Master would lead to the harmonizing of all differences, bringing the disciples into unity, till they would be of one mind and one judgment."[2]

"God does not stand toward the sinner as an executioner of the sentence against transgression; but He leaves the rejecters of His mercy to themselves to reap that which they have sown."[3]

The next in this series of studies will focus on stories Jesus told as given in the Gospels.

---

1. Ellen G. White, *Letter 83, 1895 (That I May Know Him,* p. 338).

2. Ellen G. White, *The Desire of Ages* (Boise, Idaho: Pacific Press), p. 296.

3. Ellen G. White, *The Great Controversy* (Boise, Idaho: Pacific Press), p. 36.

THE STORIES JESUS TOLD

———

The Parables

Story #1—The Soils
Matthew 13:1-23

It Takes More Than a Green Thumb!

Read the story in Matthew 13:1-23.

1. Do you have a "green thumb"? What would you do if someone gave you a room full of houseplants?

2. Why do you think Jesus told a farming story? What kind of story would Jesus tell you?

3. If you were a farmer listening to Jesus, what would you be thinking?
   a. This Man speaks my language!
   b. The farmer in the story needs to be more careful where he throws his seed!
   c. I'd rather listen to Jesus than those church people any day!
   d. I wonder what He's really talking about.

4. What is the "harvest" Jesus was talking about?
   a. Reaping what you sow.
   b. Conversion.
   c. The reward God gives those who work hard.
   d. The results of preaching the gospel.

5. What is the warning implied by the plants that died?

    a. If you grow up in a bad environment, God can't help you.
    b. If you choose to ignore the gospel, you hurt yourself.
    c. If you don't love God, He will kill you.
    d. You choose the environment of your own heart.

> "The 'honest and good heart' of which the parable speaks, is not a heart without sin. . . . He has an honest heart who yields to the conviction of the Holy Spirit. . . . The good heart is a believing heart, one that has faith in the word of God."[1]

6. In your life, what contributes to:
    a. Soil along the path that causes shallow understanding?
    b. Rocky soil that prevents good roots?
    c. The thorns of worry and concern for money?
    d. The good soil of understanding?

7. In light of the opposition that Jesus was getting from the Pharisees and others, what does this parable say about the effects of Jesus' ministry at that time? What would be the advantage of telling parables that not all could understand?

> "Heretofore Christ had occasionally made use of brief illustrations that might be called parables. Now for the first time He made parables a principal vehicle for conveying truth. The Sermon on the Mount had probably been given no more than a few weeks earlier. It was now probably the autumn of A.D. 29, and across the Plain of Gennesaret, the most productive region of all Galilee, farmers could be seen sowing their winter grain."[2]

8. What aspect of this story is good news for you?

9. Which of these "farm trivia" facts would encourage you the most as you "sow" the "seed" of the gospel?
    a. Seed can germinate after being stored for centuries.
    b. A seed of grain can yield 100 times its weight.

    c. Spring wheat is planted in the fall.

    d. The crop yield cannot be determined as the seed is planted.[3]

10. How has the soil of your life changed over the last year? The last ten years? Your lifetime?

This series on the stories Jesus told will include not only the biblical references and questions for each story but also the pages in *Christ's Object Lessons* for the same parable. You will gain the greatest benefit by studying the biblical text and answering the study questions first, then reading the material by Ellen White.

The next in this series of stories is "The Unforgiving Servant," found in Matthew 18:21-35 and *Christ's Object Lessons,* pages 243-251.

---

1. Ellen G. White, *Christ's Object Lessons* (Boise, Idaho: Pacific Press), pp. 58, 59.

2. *SDA Bible Commentary,* vol. 5, p. 403.

3. *The NIV Serendipity Bible,* p. 1259.

Story #2—The Unforgiving Servant
Matthew 18:21-35
Christ's Object Lessons, pages 243-251

$3 Billion in Debt!

1. Who would be harder for you to forgive?
   a. A person who "blows it" once but otherwise lives a good life.
   b. A person who does the same little, but irritating, things over and over and who will apparently never change.

2. Why do you think Peter had to ask how many times he should forgive his brother?
   a. He thought he was being generous and wanted Jesus to see it.
   b. He wanted to know exactly what he had to do and no more.
   c. He was the type to be motivated by duty.
   d. He thought forgiveness had to be deserved.

3. What does the parable add to what Jesus had just told Peter about forgiveness?
   a. We can forgive things that God can't.
   b. No debt is too great for God to forgive.
   c. Accepting God's forgiveness will naturally make us forgiving.
   d. God acts like a king who imprisons and tortures people.
   e. Trying to live without forgiveness (both receiving it and giving it) is a self-inflicted horror.

> One talent was 6,000 times more valuable than a denarii. Since a denarii was worth a day's wages for a farm laborer (let's assume about $50), a talent would be worth the work of about twenty years ($300,000)! Assuming forty years of work in a lifetime, the unmerciful servant, then, owed the king a sum equivalent to 5,000 lifetimes of work (about three billion dollars)! The other servant, however, owed the first servant only the equivalent of about four months' work ($5,000)!

A case history (adapted from the NIV Serendipity Bible)[1]

You have been putting up with your little brother for years. When you were growing up, you had to share a bedroom, where he kept "his side" like a pigpen. He "borrowed" your clothes without asking, left the car a mess when he used it, and never thought of filling the tank with gas. Now, the two of you run the family business, but you have to keep the books, pay the bills, and come in on Sundays while he coaches a Little League team. Recently, your doctor told you that you have an ulcer, and that it is caused by deep-seated anger against your little brother.

1. What do you do?
    a. Decide it's not worth getting sick over.
    b. Complain to his wife.
    c. Call your father and tell everything.
    d. Sweep it under the rug.
    e. Have it out with him.
    f. Take off for six months and leave the business to him.
    g. Get into counseling.

2. What have you found helpful in dealing with sour relationships?
    a. Keep short accounts.
    b. Write a letter but don't mail it.
    c. Ask someone else to mediate.
    d. Have it out—right now!
    e. Sleep on it.
    f. Get away from the situation.
    g. Break off the relationship.

3. Who caused your ulcer?
   a. Your little brother did—the brat doesn't care what he puts you through!
   b. God did—He's punishing you for not being forgiving.
   c. You did—you've never accepted your brother, much less forgiven him, so you play the martyr.
   d. You did—you've never confronted your brother with his responsibility. You just kept it bottled up inside you.

4. Who is the easiest and hardest person for you to forgive?
   a. Brother/sister.
   b. Spouse.
   c. Parents/kids.
   d. Neighbor/friend.
   e. Stranger.
   f. Yourself.
   g. God.

"When the debtor pleaded with his lord for mercy, he had no true sense of the greatness of his debt. He did not realize his helplessness. He hoped to deliver himself. 'Have patience with me,' he said, 'and I will pay thee all.' So there are many who hope by their own works to merit God's favor. They do not realize their helplessness. They do not accept the grace of God as a free gift, but are trying to build themselves up in self-righteousness. Their own hearts are not broken and humbled on account of sin, and they are exacting and unforgiving toward others. Their own sins against God, compared with their brother's sins against them, are as ten thousand talents to one hundred pence—nearly one million to one; yet they dare to be unforgiving."[2]

The next in this series of stories is "The Good Samaritan," found in Luke 10:25-37 and *Christ's Object Lessons*, pages 376-389.

---

1. *The NIV Serendipity Bible*, p. 1270.
2. Ellen G. White, *Christ's Object Lessons* (Boise, Idaho: Pacific Press), pp. 245-247.

Story #3—The Good Samaritan

Luke 10:25-37

Christ's Object Lessons, pages 376-389

The Good, the Bad, and the Indifferent

1. Why do you think the "expert in the law" (Luke 10:25) wanted to test Jesus?
   a. He wanted people to see that Jesus was not as smart as the rabbis.
   b. He didn't know that eternal life is a gift.
   c. Religion was just an intellectual game to him.
   d. He liked public debate.
   e. He thought, as a Jew, he already had eternal life.

2. When put on the spot with a "test" question, I:
   a. Get angry enough to insult the questioner.
   b. Feel intimidated, so I just keep my mouth shut.
   c. Quickly get my arguments ready and squelch the questioner.
   d. Try to make friends with the questioner.
   e. Try to get the questioner to answer his own question.
   f. Give a safe answer—one that raises little controversy.

3. In which of the above ways did Jesus react? In what ways did the expert in the law react?

4. What do you think the expert in the law thought of Jesus after this incident?

5. If you could give a "Good Samaritan" award to someone today, who would it be—and why?

6. What prevents people today from being "Good Samaritans"?

> "He [Jesus] showed that our neighbor does not mean merely one of the church or faith to which we belong. It has no reference to race, color, or class distinction. Our neighbor is every person who needs our help."[1]

7. I would risk even a lawsuit in order to help someone:
   a. Because I've got to obey God no matter how much I dislike doing it.
   b. If I knew the person really needed help.
   c. Because I really like people no matter what their circumstances.
   d. As long as I knew the person was not a con artist.
   e. Because I'm the type to take risks.
   f. In extreme circumstances only. God doesn't want us to take unnecessary risks.

> "The great difference between the Jews and the Samaritans was a difference in religious belief, a question as to what constitutes true worship. . . . The Samaritan had fulfilled the command, 'Thou shalt love thy neighbor as thyself,' thus showing that he was more righteous than those by whom he was denounced."[2]

8. What do you think the Samaritan was thinking when he stopped to help the robbery victim?
   a. I hope this doesn't take too long or cost too much!
   b. I hope there are no robbers watching.
   c. I know what it's like to be helpless.
   d. I'm scared, but I can't just leave him here.

9. What response did Jesus want from the lawyer to whom He directed the parable?

    a. That he would regard non-Jews as neighbors also.

    b. That he would look for the spirit of the law and not just the letter.

    c. That he would see that Jesus fulfilled the law.

10. How many people do you know whom you could call in the middle of the night for help?

11. What needs to be done to make your church a more caring group?

12. Do you think Jesus means for us to always rescue people from problems they have created for themselves?

13. Can you see parallels between the life of Jesus and the "Good Samaritan"?

"The fact that the Samaritan was traveling in what was to him a foreign district made his deed of mercy even more noteworthy. In this district it would be likely that the unfortunate wayfarer was a Jew, a member of the race that cherished the most bitter enmity against the Samaritans. The Samaritan knew well that if he had been the wounded victim lying beside the road he could have expected no mercy from any ordinary Jew. However, the Samaritan, at considerable risk to himself from the attacks of robbers, determined to help the poor victim."[3]

The next in this series of stories is "The Great Banquet," found in Luke 14:15-24 and *Christ's Object Lessons,* pages 219-237.

---

1. Ellen G. White, *Christ's Object Lessons* (Boise, Idaho: Pacific Press), p. 376.
2. Ibid., pp. 380, 381.
3. *SDA Bible Commentary,* vol. 5, p. 783.

Story #4—The Great Banquet
Luke 14:15-24
Christ's Object Lessons, pages 219-237

Excused From the Table

1. What is the best party or dinner invitation you have ever received?

2. Have you ever had to cancel an invitation at the last minute? How did you feel?

3. Have you ever planned a party or gathering and had people "cancel out" on you? How did you feel? How did you feel when you heard the excuses?

4. With which of the excuses in the story can you most identify?
   a. "I have just bought a field." Real estate and other investments have priority.
   b. "I have just bought five yoke of oxen." Concern for making a living, security.
   c. "I just got married." Involvement in social and family activities.

"In Jewish idiomatic usage to 'eat bread in the kingdom of God' meant to enjoy the bliss of heaven. To be sure, the Pharisee's statement itself was platitudinously correct, but the spirit in which it was made and the motive that prompted it were both entirely wrong. The speaker assumed, complacently, that he was sure of an invitation."[1]

> "In Oriental lands, to decline an invitation—except where it is obviously impossible to accept—is often considered a refusal of friendship. Among some Arabs, to decline an invitation at the time of the reminder, after having accepted the original invitation, is considered a declaration of hostility."[2]

5. Notice what leads into this story in verses 13-15. What was Jesus' point in telling the banquet story?

6. What were the invited people really saying by their excuses?
   a. You should have given me more time to get ready.
   b. I've got better things to do.
   c. I never really wanted to come to the banquet in the first place.
   d. When I first heard about it I was excited, but now I'm unavailable.
   e. I don't want to be your friend.

7. What do you think of when you read about the "Great Banquet"?
   a. God's kingdom is like a party.
   b. How hard God has tried to get people into His kingdom!
   c. The great reunion feast in heaven
   d. Not knowing if I will be there
   e. The free gift of salvation

> "By the great supper [great banquet], Christ represents the blessings offered through the gospel. The provision is nothing less than Christ Himself."[3]

8. You are at the "Great Banquet" right now. How do you feel?
   a. I'm glad someone found me and gave me an invitation.
   b. I didn't want to come, but now that I'm here, I'm glad I did.
   c. I feel embarrassed because I wanted to dress better.
   d. I'm glad to be here, but I'm not sure I trust the Master yet.
   e. I'm not sure I'm really invited; it seems too good to be true.
   f. I'm sad because people I care about are not here.
   g. I think I will have to leave.

9. Which of the following describes your life ten years ago? One or two years ago? Today?

    a. I just wish I knew I had an invitation from God.

    b. I once had an invitation from God, but it's not doing me any good now.

    c. I keep hearing God repeat His invitation, but I'm not ready to commit myself yet.

    d. The only reason I'm at the party is that God didn't give up on me.

    e. God has even taken care of my excuses!

10. How can your group help you accept God's invitation?

"In a special sense Jesus Himself may be considered as the 'servant' sent to proclaim that 'all things are now ready.' In Oriental lands even today it is customary to dispatch a messenger a short time before the feast actually begins to remind the guests of their invitation. In case a guest might have forgotten about the invitation, or might not know when he was expected to appear, this would allow him time to prepare for the occasion and to reach the place designated for the banquet. In the Orient, where less attention is paid to calendars and clocks than in Western lands, such a reminder is of practical value in that it avoids embarrassment to both the host and his guests."[4]

The next in this series of stories is "The Lost Son," found in Luke 15:11-32 and *Christ's Object Lessons,* pages 198-211.

---

1. *SDA Bible Commentary,* vol. 5, p. 808.
2. Ibid.

Story #5—The Lost Son

Luke 15:11-32
Christ's Object Lessons, pages 198-211

Lose a Servant, Gain a Son

1. Notice the subject matter of the entire chapter. How does verse 1 set the scene for Jesus' discussion of lost things? Who do you think were the "sinners" who gathered around Jesus?

> **"All the publicans and sinners**. . . . The word 'all' may refer to the fact that wherever Jesus went during this part of His ministry the 'publicans' and 'sinners' of the region flocked to hear Him. This evidence of interest angered the scribes and Pharisees still further, for they held these classes in contempt, and were in turn shunned by them. It irritated the religious leaders that Jesus should treat these despised outcasts of society with friendliness, and that they in turn responded."[1]

2. Did you ever feel like "running away"? What did you do about it? Do you have any regrets?

3. Was there a "perfect child" and a "black sheep" in your family? Which one were you? Which one are you now?

4. What are the typical strengths and weaknesses of the oldest child? What about the youngest child? In your experience, was the oldest child

a "little adult," and did the baby of the family get away with "murder" by being cute?

    5. With whom do you now identify the most?
      a. The son who had to get away from his family in order to live his own life.
      b. The son who is always dependable and hard working.
      c. The father who gives freedom no matter how much it hurts.
      d. The hired hands who are just trying to make it from one weekend to the next.
      e. The neighbors who might like to give the father some advice about raising children.

    6. With whom do you identify at the end of the story?
      a. The son whose self-worth is gone, but is being restored.
      b. The son whose life is disrupted by the weak and undisciplined brother.
      c. The father who is willing to forgive and forget just so they can be a family again.
      d. The hired hands who get invited to the party.
      e. The neighbors who will be watching what the younger son does next!

7. What physical reminders did the father give his runaway son to assure him that he was fully accepted as a son again? How has God done this for you? What can a church family do for the "lost sons and daughters" who want to come back?

8. What is the hardest thing about returning to God? To your church?

9. What is the hardest thing about growing up "in the faith" and staying a faithful church member?

10. What does this story tell you about God's attitude toward spiritual runaways?

    11. What does this story tell you about the "lost"?
      a. They are condemned to suffer in hell fire.

  b. They suffer the natural results of their choices.
  c. They go through probation when they decide to return.
  d. They may not be any further from God than those represented by the older brother.
  e. All God wants is a reunion.
  f. No one has to talk the Father into loving any of His children.

> "**Keratia** [*'husks' or 'pods'*] is used to describe the pods of the *keratea,* the carob, or locust, tree because of the hornlike shape of the pods. The pod of this tree has also been called St.-John's-bread, on the tradition that this was part of the diet of John the Baptist. After the removal of the seeds for human consumption, the pods themselves were commonly used as fodder for domestic animals—as contemporary Jewish literature often observed. The carob tree is still cultivated in Palestine, and has been introduced into the United States."[2]

"He [the elder brother] makes it plain that his own service has been that of a servant rather than a son. When he should have found an abiding joy in his father's presence, his mind has rested upon the profit to accrue from his circumspect life. His words show that it is for this he has foregone the pleasures of sin."[3]

"Self-righteousness not only leads men to misrepresent God, but makes them coldhearted and critical toward their brethren. The elder son, in his selfishness and jealousy, stood ready to watch his brother, to criticize every action, and to accuse him for the least deficiency."[4]

The next in this series of stories is "Laborers in the Vineyard," found in Matthew 20:1-16 and *Christ's Object Lessons,* pages 390-404.

---

1. *SDA Bible Commentary,* vol. 5, p. 814.
2. Ibid., p. 819.
3. Ellen G. White, *Christ's Object Lessons* (Boise, Idaho: Pacific Press), pp. 207, 208.
4. Ibid., p. 210.

Story #6—Laborers in the Vineyard
Matthew 20:1-16
Christ's Object Lessons, pages 390-404

What if God Were Only Fair?

1. What kind of people would you like to have work for you?
   a. A detail-oriented person who takes exact orders?
   b. Someone who understands the big picture and doesn't need directions.
   c. A creative person who does things you hadn't thought of.
   d. Someone who gives 110 percent but who expects promotions.
   e. Someone who is satisfied where they are.

2. What makes work "hard"?

3. On what basis do you like to be paid?
   a. Time—the longer you work, the more you get paid.
   b. Stress factors—emotionally draining work is worth more.
   c. Creativity—artistic and innovative work is rewarded.
   d. Physical demands—hard physical work deserves more pay.
   e. Value to employer—employer's profit shared with workers regardless of factors a, b, c, or d.
   f. Gift or inheritance—payment not based on performance.

4. On what basis did the following workers think they were being hired?
   a. Those hired early in the morning.

b. Those hired at various hours during the day.
c. Those hired just an hour before quitting time.

> "The truth of God's free grace had been almost lost sight of by the Jews. The rabbis taught that God's favor must be earned. The reward of the righteous they hoped to gain by their own works. Thus their worship was prompted by a grasping, mercenary spirit. From this spirit even the disciples of Christ were not wholly free, and the Saviour sought every opportunity of showing them their error."[1]

5. What is a fair wage?
    a. The same thing everyone else is getting.
    b. The amount agreed upon, no more, no less.
    c. Anything equal to or greater than what was agreed upon.
    d. Whatever meets the basic needs of food, clothes, and shelter.
    e. _______________________________________ .

6. If you were a landowner listening to Jesus, what would you have thought?
    a. Jesus would make a poor manager.
    b. Labor disputes result when you give some people more than they deserve.
    c. It's hard to find good help late in the day.
    d. Some workers are never happy.
    e. _______________________________________ .

> "The first and the last are to be sharers in the great, eternal reward, and the first should gladly welcome the last. He who grudges the reward to another forgets that he himself is saved by grace alone. The parable of the laborers rebukes all jealousy and suspicion. Love rejoices in the truth and institutes no envious comparisons. He who possesses love compares only the loveliness of Christ and his own imperfect character."[2]

7. If you were a worker listening to Jesus, what would you have thought?
   a. What a stupid landowner!
   b. What a generous landowner!
   c. It's better to work all day and be secure.
   d. If you want to feel satisfied, don't worry about what the others are getting!
   e. I'd like to work for a guy like that!

8. What is Jesus really saying:
   a. To those who grew up in the church?
   b. To those who have just been converted?
   c. To you?

9. What did the workers who were hired for only one hour miss? How does their experience illustrate "grace"? How does the attitude of the other workers illustrate "righteousness by works"?

10. What do we miss if we intentionally wait until the "eleventh hour" to answer God's call?

"The Lord desires us to rest in Him without a question as to our measure of reward. When Christ abides in the soul, the thought of reward is not uppermost. This is not the motive that actuates our service. It is true that in a subordinate sense we should have respect to the recompense of the reward. God desires us to appreciate His promised blessings. But He would not have us eager for rewards nor feel that for every duty we must receive compensation. We should not be so anxious to gain the reward as to do what is right, irrespective of all gain. Love to God and to our fellow men should be our motive."[3]

The next in this series of stories is "The Ten Maidens," found in Matthew 25:1-13 and *Christ's Object Lessons,* pages 405-421.

---

1. Ellen G. White, *Christ's Object Lessons* (Boise, Idaho: Pacific Press), p. 390.
2. Ibid., p. 402.
3. Ibid., pp. 398, 399.

Story #7—The Ten Maidens
Matthew 25:1-13
Christ's Object Lessons, pages 405-421

The Oil Crisis

1. When people I care about keep me waiting, I:
    a. Get very uptight because I have a busy schedule.
    b. Get angrier by the second.
    c. Wait five minutes and then leave.
    d. Relax and do some reading, thinking, or visiting.
    e. Calmly replan my day.
    f. Change friends.

2. Since chapters 24 and 25 are about "the end," why would Jesus tell a story about a late bridegroom?
    a. People in this Middle Eastern culture were not clock watchers and were used to waiting a lot. They would identify with the story.
    b. Jesus knew His second coming was not near, by human standards.
    c. Preparing for the second coming is like preparing for a wedding.
    d. Just because the bridegroom seems late doesn't mean the wedding is off.
    e. Being patient and being prepared are more important than believing in a soon coming.
    f. ____ .

> "The two classes of watchers represent the two classes who profess to be waiting for their Lord. They are called virgins because they profess a pure faith. By the lamps is represented the word of God. The psalmist says, 'Thy word is a lamp unto my feet, and a light unto my path.' Ps. 119:105. The oil is a symbol of the Holy Spirit. Thus the Spirit is represented in the prophecy of Zechariah."[1]

3. Why do you think the five foolish maidens didn't bring enough oil?
   a. They were so excited they forgot to plan ahead.
   b. They couldn't imagine the groom being so late.
   c. They didn't really know the groom.
   d. They knew the groom was coming soon and didn't need to know anything else.

   e. ____.

4. How long have you believed that Jesus is coming "soon"? How has your understanding of "soon" matured since you first believed?

> "It is the darkness of misapprehension of God that is enshrouding the world. Men are losing their knowledge of His character. It has been misunderstood and misinterpreted. At this time a message from God is to be proclaimed, a message illuminating in its influence and saving in its power. His character is to be made known."[2]
>
> "The grace of God has been freely offered to every soul. . . . But character is not transferable. No man can believe for another. No man can receive the Spirit for another."[3]

5. Have you ever felt betrayed by God because He hasn't come yet? How have you dealt with those feelings?

6. Jesus wants me to understand this story because:
   a. He knows I'm likely to be frustrated when things don't happen on schedule.

b. His heart goes out to those who are so tired of waiting for Him that they fall asleep.

c. While my religious feelings go up and down, only He can supply the "oil" to get me through to the end.

d. He doesn't want to come and find me out "shopping."

7. What significance do you see in the fact that *all* the maidens slept?

8. What kind of preparation will make us ready to meet Jesus? How does your answer fit in with being saved by grace?

9. What does verse 12 tell you about who is saved and who is lost?

"The Spirit works upon man's heart, according to his desire and consent implanting in him a new nature; but the class represented by the foolish virgins have been content with a superficial work. They do not know God. They have not studied His character; they have not held communion with Him; therefore they do not know how to trust, how to look and live."[4]

The next in this series of stories is "The Talents," found in Matthew 25:14-30 and *Christ's Object Lessons,* pages 325-365.

---

1. Ellen G. White, *Christ's Object Lessons* (Boise, Idaho: Pacific Press), p. 406.
2. Ibid., p. 415.
3. Ibid., p. 412.
4. Ibid., p. 411.

Story #8—The Talents
Matthew 25:14-30
Christ's Object Lessons, page 325-365

High Yield or No Risk?

> "Remember that you will never reach a higher standard than you yourself set."[1]

1. When you were a kid, who was the most talented person in your class? Were you ever jealous? What is that person doing now?

2. What is one talent you wish you had been born with? How can you enjoy or appreciate this talent in others?

3. What talents do you see in the members of your group? (While one member is silent, other members talk about the capabilities of this person. Do this for each member of your group.)

4. How do you feel after having people recognize your talents?

5. Are you hesitant to say that you are good at something?

6. Was the master in the story fair to his servants?

7. Who took the most risk and the least risk?
   a. The master.
   b. The five-talent servant.

    c. The two-talent servant.
    d. The one-talent servant.

> "God will accept only those who are determined to aim high. He places every human agent under obligation to do his best. . . . We need to understand that imperfection of character is sin. All righteous attributes of character dwell in God as a perfect, harmonious whole, and everyone who receives Christ as a personal Saviour is privileged to possess these attributes."[2]

8. Which servant is most like your natural temperament?
    a. The five-talent servant. I'm ready to tackle anything. No challenge is too great, and I follow through until I get results.
    b. The two-talent servant. I'm a bit more cautious than the five-talent servant. I know my limits, but I get results.
    c. The one-talent servant. I doubt if I can get results, so I'm afraid to try anything.

> "The question that most concerns us is not, How much have I received? but, What am I doing with that which I have? The development of all our powers is the first duty we owe to God and to our fellow men. No one who is not growing daily in capability and usefulness is fulfilling the purpose of his life."[3]

9. What kind of reward did the master give the first two servants? What does this say about the master's motives?

10. What do you think of the one-talent servant's excuses for not investing?
    a. He was just trying to cover up his laziness.
    b. He thought he had done the only safe thing.
    c. His fear of the master had paralyzed him.
    d. His fear of failure had paralyzed him.
    e. The master expected too much of him.
    f. ___________________________________ .

11. How have you misunderstood God in the past? How does being scared of God stunt your growth?

12. Can you see a relationship between knowing what kind of person God is (knowing His goals and motives) and developing your talents?

13. Why did Jesus include this parable in His discourse on the end time?

> "From the beginning it has been Satan's studied plan to cause men to forget God, that he might secure them to himself. Hence he has sought to misrepresent the character of God, to lead men to cherish a false conception of Him. The Creator has been presented to their minds as clothed with the attributes of the prince of evil himself,—as arbitrary, severe, and unforgiving,—that He might be feared, shunned, and even hated by men. Satan hoped to so confuse the minds of those whom he had deceived that they would put God out of their knowledge."[4]

The next series of studies will focus on the growing church as described in the book of Acts.

---

1. Ellen G. White, *Christ's Object Lessons* (Boise, Idaho: Pacific Press), p. 331.
2. Ibid., p. 330.
3. Ibid., pp. 329, 330.
4. Ellen G. White, *Testimonies for the Church* (Boise, Idaho: Pacific Press), vol. 5, p. 738.

STORIES

of a

GROWING

CHURCH

Acts

Story #1 Acts 1, 2
—Jesus ascends
—The apostles
—Pentecost

Planting the Church

Acts 1:1-11

For the following questions, pretend you are one of the apostles having just seen Jesus go up into heaven.

1. Remembering what Jesus said before He left, what will you be doing in the near future?

2. How will this affect your family?

3. How long do you think it will be before Jesus returns?

Now go back and answer the same questions from your own twentieth-century perspective.

Acts 1:12-26

4. What were the qualifications of an apostle? Why couldn't the church just choose any sincere believer to be an apostle?

5. How do you know Jesus was resurrected? React to the diagram on page 70 that outlines several possibilities regarding Jesus' tomb on Easter morning.

6. Do you think the apostles believed without evidence? Does having more faith mean we should demand less evidence?

Acts 2

7. How do you feel when someone makes fun of what you believe? Can you briefly describe a personal experience in which this happened?

8. Compared to what Peter was like before Jesus' death, do you see a change in his thoughts and behavior in Acts chapters 1 and 2?

9. How has your Christian growth been like Peter's? How has it been different?

10. The following are factors that contributed to the rapid growth of the early church. How can we apply these today?
   a. The Holy Spirit initiated preaching and hearing. Result: 3,000 added (see Acts 2:41).
   b. The spiritual life of the church members included apostles' teaching, fellowship, breaking of bread, and prayer. Result: numbers added daily (see Acts 2:47).

11. After you have read the entire books of Acts, what title would you give it?

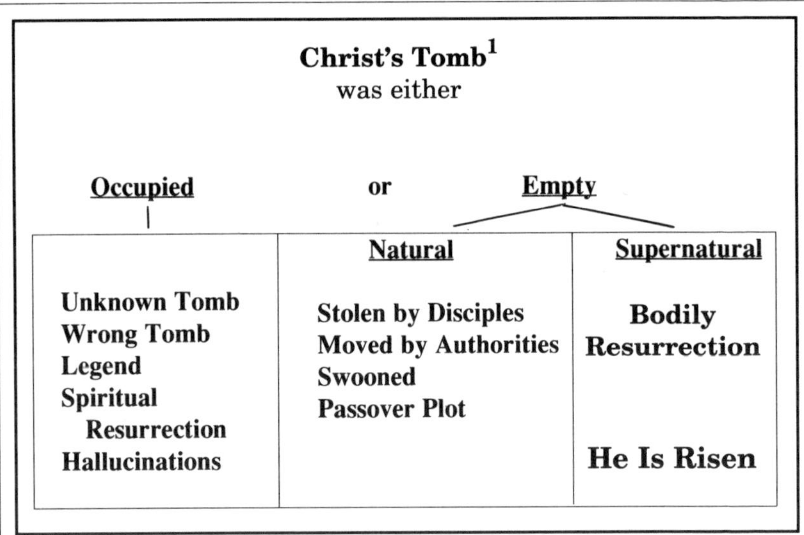

The next in this series of Bible stories is found in Acts chapters 3-5.

---

1. Josh McDowell, *The Resurrection Factor* (San Bernardino, Calif.: Here's Life Publishers, 1981), p. 102.

Story #2 Acts 3, 4, 5
—Beggar healed
—Peter and John imprisoned

Removing the Barriers

Acts 3

1. Have you ever asked God for a miracle?

2. Does God grant miracles based on the "godliness" of the person asking? Does God grant miracles based on a person's faith?

3. From Peter's explanation, can you tell why God healed the beggar?

4. Can you think of a reason for God not performing a miracle even though a person had great faith?

> **Solomon's colonnade (Acts 3:11).** "The porch that ran along the east side of the Court of the Gentiles. It had rows of 27-foot-high stone columns and a roof of cedar. It was a good thirty yards wide and over five hundred yards long, so there was plenty of room for large gatherings (5:12)."[1]

Acts 4:1-31

5. Notice Peter's statement in Acts 2:21 that quotes from Joel 2. How do you think the Jewish leaders reacted to Peter's statement in Acts 4:12?

6. Can you relate to the reaction of Peter and John in Acts 4:20?

7. If I were asked, right now, to testify in a hostile court about my belief in Christ, I would:
a. Ask to see a good lawyer.
b. Refuse to testify on the grounds it might incriminate me.
c. Be so nervous I would have a hard time speaking.
d. Ask for a phone call so I could call my pastor.
e. Rejoice for such an opportunity.

8. Was the transformation of Peter instantaneous or gradual?

> **Stone (Acts 4:11).** "The apostles are technically on their defence, but actually they have gone over to the attack; Peter proceeds to preach the gospel to his judges, and he does so by citing a well-known OT scripture. 'The stone which the builders rejected is become the head of the corner' (Ps. 118:22) is one of the earliest messianic testimonies."[2]

Acts 4:32–5:11

9. Even though the believers were of "one heart and mind" about sharing, do you think this was a church policy or a requirement given by the apostles?

> **Church (Acts 5:11).** This is the first time that the word *church* (Greek *ekklesia*) occurs in Acts. While the Greeks used the word to denote a citizen-assembly of a Greek city,[3] the Septuagint (Greek translation of the Old Testament) uses this word (translated "congregation" in many English Bibles) to refer to the nation of Israel. The book of Acts applies this Jewish usage to the new community of people who believed in Jesus as the Messiah.

Acts 5:12-42

10. Imagine you are Peter leaving the Sanhedrin, rejoicing after being mistreated. How did God bring you to this level of maturity?

(Think of specific events in Peter's past with which you can identify.)

The next in this series of Bible stories is found in Acts chapters 6-9.

1. *Acts,* Life Change Series (Colorado Springs: NavPress, 1987), p. 49.
2. F. F. Bruce, *The Book of Acts, The New International Commentary on the New Testament* (Grand Rapids, Mich.: Eerdmans, 1975), p. 99.
3. Ibid., p. 116.

Story #3 Acts 6-9

—Stephen stoned
—Persecution
—Saul converted

Transition

Acts 6

1. What might have happened if the apostles had not delegated leadership to others?

2. Do you think it was an inferior position to "wait on tables"? Is that all the chosen seven did?

3. What was the benefit from choosing the seven?

4. What surprises you most about verse 7?

5. Delegation of leadership helped the early church grow. How can we use this principle to promote growth in our church?

> **Ministry (Acts 1:25).** "The Greek word *diakonia* means 'service' (originally service at a meal table), and it is used of Christian work of all kinds, which takes its pattern from the One who came not to be served but to serve (Mark 10:45). 'To serve tables' in Acts 6:2 (NASB) is *diakonoi;* this is the root of the English word *deacon.*"[1]

Acts 7

6. Why do you think Stephen ended up in more trouble than the twelve apostles? What about his ethnic identity? What about his speech to the Sanhedrin?

7. How can persecution be a good thing? Is God the cause of persecution?

Acts 8

8. What does the story of Simon tell us about miracles? Is the miraculous always of God? Does God give miracles for proof?

9. The story of Philip shows the rite of baptism to be a natural response to understanding the gospel. If you have been baptized, tell the group how you felt at the time and how you feel about it now. If you have not been baptized, tell the group your feelings about preparing for it.

Acts 9

10. Find Jerusalem and Damascus on a map. Why do you think Saul was so dedicated that he would go all the way to Damascus to find Christians?

11. How do you think Saul proved that "Jesus is the Christ" in verse 22? React to the diagram on page 77—Jesus' Claims to Be God.

12. What does verse 27 tell you about the kind of person Barnabas was?

13. When I am confronted with new spiritual information, I usually:
    a. Accept it immediately.
    b. Wait a while and think about it.
    c. Tend to rely on what I know already.
    d. Reject it at first, then reconsider.
    e. I don't know; I haven't heard anything new in a long time.
    f. Make a decision based on how much I have to change my life.
    g. ____.

14. How can times of peace be beneficial to a church?

15. Notice the reaction to miracles in verse 35. Does our society react differently today? Is that good or bad? Does the Holy Spirit work differently today?

> **The Son of God (Acts 9:20).** "This is the only instance where the title is used of Jesus in Acts. What Paul proclaimed was (1) that Christ was verily the Son of God no less than the son of David, (2) that Jesus of Nazareth had been shown to be the Christ. Not only was this a perplexity to the Jews, but it seemed to them a blasphemous claim."[2]

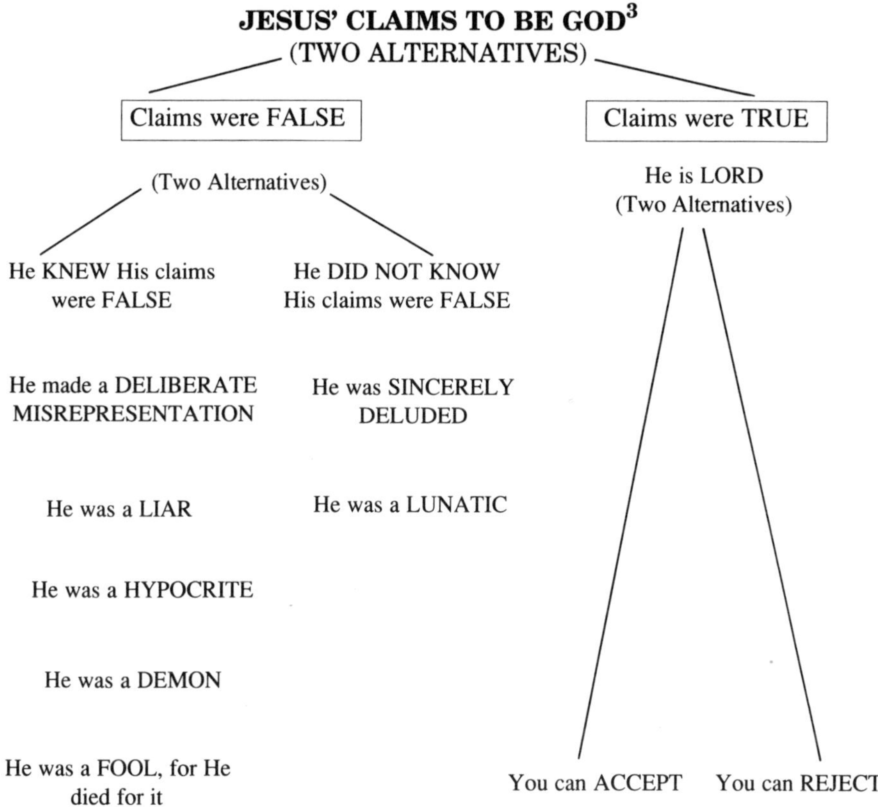

The next in this series of Bible stories is found in Acts chapters 10-12.

1. *Acts,* Life Change Series (Colorado Springs: NavPress, 1987), p. 26.

2. *Seventh-day Adventist Bible Commentary,* vol. 6, p. 234.

3. Josh McDowell, *Evidence That Demands a Verdict* (Campus Crusade for Christ, 1972), p. 108.

Story #4 Acts 10, 11, 12
—Peter and Cornelius
—Peter imprisoned

Beyond the Old Limits

Acts 10:1–11:18

1. What were the outward signs of Cornelius's spiritual experience?

2. From what you know of Jewish dietary laws, can you sympathize with the dilemma the vision first presented to Peter? Notice verse 14.

3. When Peter understood the meaning of the vision, he changed:
   a. His mind about what he wanted for lunch.
   b. His attitude about Roman soldiers.
   c. His relationship to non-Jews.
   d. His evangelistic strategy.
   e. His practice of taking a nap before lunch.

4. What purpose does the gift of tongues seem to serve in verses 44-47 (see also Acts 11:17)?

Acts 11:19-30

5. Notice how this section completes the transition from a church of only Jewish converts to a church with a world mission. Do you think some of the Jewish Christians felt threatened by this transition? What can we learn from this?

Centurion (Acts 10:1). "The commander of a century, about a hundred soldiers. There were six centuries in a cohort and ten cohorts in a legion. Thus, Cornelius was roughly equivalent to a sergeant major or a captain over a company. Commanders of legions and cohorts were generally aristocrats who served for a year or two on their way to high civilian office, but centurions were career military men chosen for talent and character. They provided the stability that made the Roman army strong."[1]

The circumcised believers (Acts 11:2). For Peter to enter a Gentile house was a revolutionary act and aroused alarm among the "circumcised." These were a group of "Jewish believers who were specially zealous for the law" and sticklers for the ban on social intercourse between Jews and Gentiles.[2]

Being zealous for the law was undoubtedly one of the reasons the Jerusalem believers were held in high esteem by the populace. For a prominent person of their number, such as Peter, to do such a rash thing might endanger their standing in the community. Besides, their inherently conservative natures (compared to the Hellenistic Christians) would react negatively to such a "progressive" step as fraternizing with Gentiles.

Acts 12

6. How was Herod's motive for persecuting Christians different from Saul's in Acts 9? Did Herod have any personal animosity toward Christians? Do you think that made Herod more or less dangerous to the Christian population?

7. Would Peter's faith have been any less valid had God allowed him to be executed?

8. Notice verse 17. Earlier when Peter had been released from prison, he stayed in Jerusalem (see Acts 4). Why didn't he do so this time? Does your answer to question #6 relate to your answer to this question?

9. What effect did Peter's escape have on Herod? What effect do you think God wanted it to have? Did God harden Herod's heart? How?

10. How do we decide whether to do everything we can to avoid persecution or to initiate confrontation no matter what the consequences?

The next in this series of Bible stories is found in Acts chapters 13-16.

---

1. *Acts,* Life Change Series (Colorado Springs: NavPress, 1987), p. 106.
2. F. F. Bruce, *The Book of Acts, The New International Commentary on the New Testament* (Grand Rapids, Mich.: Eerdmans, 1975), p. 234.

Story #5 Acts 13-16
—Paul and Barnabas
—Paul and Silas

Team Efforts

Acts 13

1. From what you know about Saul (Paul) and Barnabas, explain why the Holy Spirit chose them as a team.

> **Desired a king (Acts 13:21).** "In doing so, the ancestors of Paul's Jewish hearers had rejected God (1 Sam. 8:7). The apostle was soon to tell them (Acts 13:23-28) that their fellow country-men had also rejected Jesus as the Messiah. The expectation of a kingly Messiah, for whom the Jews of Paul's day looked in vain, had caused them to commit a sin similar to that of their fore-fathers."[1]

2. Paul and Barnabas seem to have had opposite personality traits, yet they were both valuable in the spreading of the gospel. Have one of your group sit silently while the rest describe how he or she is like Paul or Barnabas. Tell how this person is valuable in the spread of the gospel. Go around the circle until each person has had a turn being the silent subject.

3. Imagine yourself to be a Gentile listening to Paul's speech in verses 16-41. What does Paul say that appeals to you? What parts of the

speech would impress you if you were Jewish?

Acts 14

4. What made the words Paul and Barnabas spoke so effective? Facts? Logic? Emotional content? How do you think Paul's rabbinical training helped him?

> **God-fearing women of high standing (Acts 13:50).** "Judaism was especially attractive to Gentile women of the middle and upper classes. These women had enough wealth, education, and leisure to feel that traditional religion and social relations were unfulfilling. According to their various temperaments, dissatisfied women flocked either to Judaism or to the oriental cults. It was easier for a woman than a man to become a Jew, since women did not have to undergo circumcision."[2]

5. The story in Acts 14:8-20 shows how human nature tends to either put heroes up on a pedestal where they don't belong or to treat them as scapegoats. How do we see this tendency in our society today? How are Christians tempted in these areas?

Acts 15

6. How do you see church organization contributing to church growth?

7. How did Paul relate to the decision of the majority at the Jerusalem council? Is there a lesson here?

8. Why didn't the Holy Spirit settle all the disputes in the early church?

Acts 16

9. Why did Paul circumcise Timothy? What can we learn from Timothy's example. How do you feel about doing something for the sake of others that you don't want to do?

10. Does Paul's example in Acts 16:18 encourage us to look for

confrontations with evil spirits? Have you ever been in what you felt was a direct or indirect confrontation with an evil power? If so, was your faith strengthened?

11. How do you feel about the reaction of Paul and Silas when unjustly put in jail? What about their reaction when they were released?

12. How do we know when to suffer gladly and when to demand justice?

The next in this series of Bible stories is found in Acts chapters 17-20.

---

1. *Seventh-day Adventist Bible Commentary,* vol. 6, p. 287.
2. *Acts,* Life Change Series (Colorado Springs: NavPress, 1987), pp. 119, 120.

Story #6 Acts 17-20

—Thessalonica, Berea, Athens, and Corinth
—Ephesus, Macedonia, Greece, and Troas

To the World

Acts 17

1. Notice how Paul made use of the Sabbath synagogue services wherever he went. Do you think Paul thought of his activity as anti-Jewish? Was he consciously starting a new religion?

2. In what way was the charge against Christians in verse 7 similar to the charge against Jesus at His trial?

3. Notice verse 21. What is beneficial, and what might not be beneficial, about the Athenians' hunger for new ideas?

4. Do you think Paul's speech in the Areopagus at Athens was the same as the speeches he gave in the synagogues? Why?

> **Areopagus (Acts 17:19).** " 'Hill of Ares,' *Ares* being the Greek equivalent to the Latin *Mars,* the god of war; hence, *Areios Pagos* is translated 'Mar's hill' in v. 22."[1]

Acts 18

5. Notice verses 9 and 10. How might this assurance be applied to us today? Does it mean we will never be harmed?

> **Men of Athens (Acts 17:22).** "Although this is a respectful opening, the speech that follows is not that of a man on trial, but of an ardent advocate of peculiar, but cherished, beliefs. Paul adopts the language of Athenian orators. This was in keeping with his custom of adapting himself to his audience. That Paul was able to do this speaks highly of his ability."[2]

6. Notice the role of argument and debate in spreading the gospel. What does this say about the relationship of faith and evidence?

Acts 19

7. Why was it necessary for some disciples to be rebaptized?

8. Do you find it interesting that Paul didn't build any church buildings? Why didn't he need to?

9. What does the story of the seven sons of Sceva teach us? In what way can fear (verse 17) be a good thing?

10. Relate verse 32 to today.

> **Jews who went around driving out evil spirits (Acts 19:13).** "Among practitioners of magic in ancient times Jews enjoyed high respect, for they were believed to have specially effective spells at their command. In particular, the fact that the name of the God of Israel was not to be pronounced by vulgar lips was generally known among the pagans, and misinterpreted by them according to regular magical principles."[3]

Acts 20

11. Does it seem contradictory that Paul was warned by the Spirit (verse 23) about going to Jerusalem and yet "compelled" by the Spirit (verse 22) to go to that very place?

12. Does God always have just one plan for our lives, or are there multiple options within His will?

The next in this series of Bible stories is found in Acts chapters 21-24.

1. *Seventh-day Adventist Bible Commentary,* vol. 6, p. 349.
2. Ibid., p. 350.
3. F. F. Bruce, *The Book of Acts, The New International Commentary on the New Testament* (Grand Rapids, Mich.: Eerdmans, 1975), p. 390.

Story #7 Acts 21-24
—Paul arrested
—Before the Sanhedrin
—Death plot and transfer to Caesarea

Faith on Trial

Acts 21

1. Verses 10-14 seem to be the final warning to Paul against going to Jerusalem. How would you have felt had you been one of Paul's close friends or family members?

2. Can friends and family actually hinder God's work? Notice verse 13.

3. Can you understand the administrative problem facing James and the elders concerning Paul's reputation? Did Paul seem to mind doing something in order to avoid controversy?

> **Philip the evangelist (Acts 21:9).** "By this time, Philip had a flourishing family of four daughters, a credit to their father, for they all had the gift of prophecy. Several years later Philip and his daughters, with other Palestinian Christians, migrated to the province of Asia, and spent their remaining days there. . . . The daughters, or at least some of them, lived to a great age, and were highly esteemed as informants on persons and events belonging to the early years of Judaean Christianity."[1]

4. Notice verse 24. The elders wanted the people to think Paul was living in obedience to the law. Was this the truth? Was it OK for the Gentile believers not to live in obedience to the law?

> **Aramaic (Acts 21:40; 22:2).** "The Greek word could mean Hebrew (NASB, KJV), but Aramaic was the common langauge of the people. The two languages were related, so the people could have understood Hebrew with some effort (like modern people hearing a man speak King James English). Because many Jews outside Palestine could not speak Aramaic or Hebrew, Paul was identifying himself with his audience of patriotic, conservative Palestinian Jews by using their ancestral language."[2]

Acts 22

5. How did Paul's conversion story affect the crowd? Did they want to flog him for religious reasons?

6. How do you relate to Paul's conversion story?

Acts 23

7. Was Paul correct, or incorrect, when he called the high priest a "whitewashed wall"? Was Paul right in saying that?

8. Why did the Pharisees suddenly become Paul's allies?

9. Why did Paul need to hear what the Lord told him in verse 11?

Acts 24

10. What, in this chapter, indicates that Paul did not consider Christianity to be a new religion?

11. It's one thing to be criticized for something you actually believe or do. It's quite another thing to be on trial over a misunderstanding of motives—or simply due to prejudice. How would you apply Paul's example in this area to your life?

The next in this series of Bible stories is found in Acts chapters 25-28.

---

1. F. F. Bruce, *The Book of Acts, The New International Commentary on the New Testament* (Grand Rapids, Mich.: Eerdmans, 1975), p. 424.
2. *Acts,* Life Change Series (Colorado Springs: NavPress, 1987), p. 182.

Story #8 Acts 25-28

—Trial by Festus and Agrippa

—The trip to Rome

—Advancing the gospel

True to the Vision

Acts 25

1. Put yourself in Paul's place. Why did he appeal to Caesar? With which of the following reasons would you identify most?

    a. He had been in prison so long he figured this would accomplish something.

    b. He thought Caesar would give him a fair trial and that the Jews wouldn't.

    c. Anything to keep from having to go back to Jerusalem!

    d. God said he would witness in Rome. Appealing to Caesar would get him there.

    e. ____.

I appeal to Caesar! (Acts 25:11). "Felix had been an experienced administrator of Judaea when Paul's case was submitted to him, but Festus was a novice, and his inexperience might well be exploited [by the Sanhedrin] to Paul's detriment. There was one way open to Paul as a Roman citizen to escape from this precarious situation, even if it was a way attended by special risks of its own."[1]

> **Agrippa (Acts 25:13, 14).** Agrippa the younger had the reputation of being an authority on the Jewish religion, and Festus decided that he was the man who could best help him to frame the report which he had to submit to Rome in connection with Paul's appeal to the emperor.[2]

Acts 26

2. Can you remember when you first came to grips with the meaning of the resurrection? What difference has it made in your life? Try to think of something recent to tell the group.

3. This chapter contains the third account of Paul's conversion. Why would Luke, the author of Acts, write it down so completely three times?

4. In verse 19, Paul says, "I was not disobedient to the vision from heaven." Has God given you a vision, an insight into His plan for you?

5. Paul was defending himself. What other effect was his speech having? Notice verse 28. What effect does it have on you?

Acts 27

6. Have there been "storms" in your life that have nearly destroyed you? Has God brought good out of bad situations in your life, even when you made a bad decision that brought on the situation?

Acts 28

7. What evidence would Paul cite from his life to show that God's plan cannot fail?

8. What was Paul's attitude toward the Jews in Rome? What was their attitude toward him at first, and then later? How does Paul's attitude illustrate God's attitude toward us?

Further Reflection

9. How do you feel about the evidence that the Holy Spirit is working in your life?

> **"This closes the biblical history of the early church.** If Luke wrote a further account, it is no longer extant. For the years following Paul's release and for his second imprisonment and death we have only hints in the so-called pastoral epistles, 1 Timothy, 2 Timothy, and Titus, and in early Christian tradition."[3]

"During Paul's final trial before Nero, the emperor had been so strongly impressed with the force of the apostle's words that he deferred the decision of the case, neither acquitting nor condemning the accused servant of God. But the emperor's malice against Paul soon returned. Exasperated by his inability to check the spread of the Christian religion, even in the imperial household, he determined that as soon as a plausible pretext could be found, the apostle should be put to death. Not long afterward Nero pronounced the decision that condemned Paul to a martyr's death. Inasmuch as a Roman citizen could not be subjected to torture, he was sentenced to be beheaded.

"Paul was taken in a private manner to the place of execution. Few spectators were allowed to be present; for his persecutors, alarmed at the extent of his influence, feared that converts might be won to Christianity by the scenes of his death. But even the hardened soldiers who attended him listened to his words and with amazement saw him cheerful and even joyous in the prospect of death. To some who witnessed his martyrdom, his spirit of forgiveness toward his murderers and his unwavering confidence in Christ till the last, proved a savor of life unto life. More than one accepted the Saviour whom Paul preached, and erelong fearlessly sealed their faith with their blood."[4]

1. F. F. Bruce, *The Book of Acts, The New International Commentary on the New Testament* (Grand Rapids, Mich.: Eerdmans, 1975), p. 447.
2. Ibid., p. 482.
3. *Seventh-day Adventist Bible Commentary,* vol. 6, p. 464.
4. Ellen G. White, *The Acts of the Apostles* (Boise, Idaho: Pacific Press), p. 509.

How Did the Spirit Grow a Church?

Church Growth Principles From the Book of Acts

> This study reviews the book of Acts from the perspective of church growth. Ask yourself the following: What did the early church do that enabled it to grow? Since the book of Acts could actually be called the "Acts of the Holy Spirit," another way of asking the question is: In what specific ways did the Holy Spirit bring about growth in the early church that are applicable today?
>
> This study lists seven major principles that may give us a start in answering these questions.

1. The Holy Spirit initiated preaching and hearing (Acts 2). On the day of Pentecost, the Holy Spirit worked on both speaker and hearer!

> *Result:* Three thousand converts were added to the church (see Acts 2:41).

2. The devotional life of the church members (see Acts 2:42) included:
   a. Apostles' teaching—the good news about Jesus.
   b. Fellowship—meeting in large and small groups.
   c. Breaking of bread—spiritual and social interaction.
   d. Prayer—the same link to heaven that Jesus had.

Result: The Lord added to their number daily.

3. Freewill sharing of property (see Acts 4:32–5:11). This was not a church policy or rule, rather, a freewill response to the gospel. Insincerity, however, was exposed and punished by God.

Result: There were no needy among them (see Acts 4:34).

4. Leadership shared and delegated (see Acts 6:2). The apostles were dedicated to the ministry of the Word and prayer. Others were ordained to "wait tables." Those "waiting tables" also engaged in debating and missionary activities. Stephen was the first martyr, and Philip was known as an evangelist.

Result: The Word of God spread, the number of disciples increased rapidly, and a large number of priests were obedient (see Acts 6:7).

5. Church organization (see Acts 16:4). Even Paul, rather than asserting dictatorial power, used a delegation process to form church policy. The decision of the Jerusalem Council was given to all the churches.

Result: The churches were strengthened in the faith and grew daily in numbers.

6. God's power over evil (see Acts 19:14). In spite of facing devils, beatings, or imprisonment, the apostles went forward, knowing that God's plan cannot fail.

Result: "The word of the Lord spread widely and grew in power" (Acts 19:20).

7. Follow the vision (see Acts 26:19). Paul was not disobedient to his vision of Jesus. In fact, he says he was "compelled by the Spirit," no matter what lay ahead (see Acts 20:22).

Result: God's plan kept going forward. Paul practically converted King Agrippa (see Acts 26:28) and ended up in Rome with freedom to preach the good news (see Acts 28:31).